Stepping Out of His Shadow

KNOW YOUR WORTH

JAMIE LEE

Jamie Lee
Stepping Out of His Shadow: Know Your Worth

Published by BooxAi
ISBN: 978-965-578-649-1

Introduction

Embarking on this journey of self-discovery and healing has been both arduous and illuminating. In just 40 days, the tumultuous relationship I found myself entangled in led to a profound awakening. While this connection was fraught with toxicity, I've come to cherish it as a vital stepping stone in my evolution.

This story unfolds as a remarkable odyssey through the labyrinth of self-identity, from unhealed wounds from past relationships to enduring emotional and verbal abuse during my marriage. I once awoke each day mired in self-loathing, my yearning for a fresh start obscured by the shadows of despair. Tears flowed endlessly after my escape from a marriage I fought relentlessly to salvage, and the weight of societal expectations nearly crushed me. But within this reflection, a question emerged: why did I place greater value on the opinions of others than on my own self-worth?

I had allowed my identity to be overshadowed by others to the point where I barely recognized myself. It was a painful awakening, and the journey to self-reclamation was nothing short of a heroic ascent. I became determined to redefine my worth, for I refused to become a statistic.

The heart of my story lies in a series of relationships marked by the gradual erosion of my identity, a loss of self under the shadows of others. The essence of my book, 'Stepping Out of His Shadow: Know Your Worth,' encapsulates this profound transformation. I share this tale not as a testament to victimhood, but as a beacon of resilience and self-empowerment.

This narrative has inspired me, and I aim to be an inspiration for those who have traversed similar, treacherous paths or continue to do so. I offer insights that transcend gender and circumstance, focusing on the invaluable journey of recognizing and nurturing one's self-worth.

Amidst the backdrop of these tumultuous relationships lies a beacon of hope, illuminating the path to healthier, more fulfilling connections. By sharing my story, I endeavor to shed light on the profound impact of trauma and abuse and offer guidance for those navigating their own path to healing and growth. This book is an embrace, a hand reached out to those who are ready to transform their pain into strength.

Part One

Situations vs. Reality

Relationship Started on Lies

A few of my past relationships started with multiple lies. One thing I never understood was why lie. Especially at the beginning of a relationship and when you first meet. What do they have to lose by telling you the truth? You had just met. Through therapy, I learned that they create a lie because they have made the decision that they like you, but are afraid you won't accept them for who they are. So, they attempt to give you a version of them that you will accept and as time goes on, the more they get to know you, they mold into the perfect partner you want them to be.

My oldest daughter's father told me when we met that he was single and that he had 3 children. He also said he owned a beautiful home with a big backyard, a pole barn, and a hot tub. He lived a little over two hours away from me. So seeing him was hard, especially with him traveling all the time for work, but we were on and off for a few months. After being intimate twice, I found out I was pregnant. When I first told him he was so excited. He went to the first baby appointment, and I thought everything was going to be great. He went ghost shortly after. I would hear from him occasionally but that threw up a red flag. I ended up finding the mother of his oldest boys on Facebook and messaged her. I told her that her boys were going to have another sibling to make a total of four kids and she informed me that our daughter was baby number seven. She proceeded to tell me that he doesn't take care of any of his kids but the one that is living with him and his girlfriend. I learned then that he didn't live at the house and address that he told me about. It was his friend's house. He lied about where he lived, his relationship status, and how many children he had.

My ex-husband did the same thing. Camari knew exactly what I went through with my first daughter's father and shamed this man for not being a father and doing what he did, just for him to turn around and do the same thing tenfold. He lied about where and who he was living with, and how many children he had. He told me he owned his own business, he claimed his mother and sister had passed away. The lies were nonstop with him. A lot of stories he told had truth to them, but he was always the victim in every story. This man has been using women for two decades for his personal gain and personal benefit. He said he had three children, and they were from his first marriage. It wasn't until after I walked away from the marriage that he had eleven children before our child together but there is potentially more that no one knows about.

In the last relationship, which was short-lived, we met on a dating site, and he told me that he and his wife separated around seven years ago and told me about another relationship he had been in for about two and a half years. When he started acting strangely again, that threw red flags for me and I did my research and it turned out he indeed was still married and still living with her under the same roof. When I brought this to his attention, he tried to explain that he was going to tell me, but he didn't have the right time to tell me. That there was yet another lie because we talked about my ex-husband and the things he put me through. You had an opportunity, multiple, but you chose not to tell me. He never intended for me to find out because when he met me, he had made his decision. He liked me and knew he wouldn't be accepted if he told me he was still married and living with her. The relationship was doomed before it ever started. After 40 days, the relationship was over. I didn't take all these years to heal, to relive the same shit with a different man.

Reality

In the beginning stages of a relationship, it is not uncommon to perceive your partner as flawless. However, it is important to recognize that in some cases, this initial perfection may be the result of being involved with a narcissist. Narcissists possess an inflated sense of self-importance and often exhibit manipulative behaviors to maintain control and dominance over their partners. These individuals tend to be highly charismatic and skilled at presenting themselves in a positive light, making it difficult for their partners to identify their true nature. It is crucial to be aware of the signs of narcissism and to prioritize self-care and emotional well-being when entering a new relationship. By maintaining a strong sense of self and setting boundaries, individuals can protect themselves from the potential harm that may arise from being involved with a narcissist.

Devil in Disguise: Love Bombing

When I met my ex-husband, he fulfilled all the criteria I had for a partner. I had complete trust in him, never questioning his whereabouts, activities, or the company he kept. It was clear where I stood in his life, as he treated me with the utmost respect and admiration. He went above and beyond, treating me like royalty and even excelling as a stepfather. This relationship brought me immense happiness and a sense of certainty. Without a doubt, I knew he was the one for me.

In my entire existence, I have never been more mistaken. This man took advantage of my willingness to open up about my past, to humiliate and inflict pain upon me. He maliciously spread my most hidden and shameful secrets. Every single aspect of my past was weaponized against me. What kind of person would do this to someone they said they loved?

Reality

Love bombing is a manipulative tactic used by individuals to gain control over their targets. It involves showering the target with excessive attention, affection, and gifts to create a sense of dependency and emotional attachment. This tactic is often employed by narcissists and other manipulative individuals to exploit the vulnerabilities of their victims. Love bombing can be extremely damaging to the target's mental and emotional well-being, as it creates an artificial sense of intimacy and trust that is later used to manipulate and control. It is important for individuals to be aware of the signs of love bombing and to set boundaries in their relationships to protect themselves from emotional manipulation.

When starting a conversation with a man, it is important to consider the characteristics you are looking for. By asking about your preferences, he can tailor his behavior accordingly. Additionally, discussing past relationships and traumas can indeed establish a deeper connection and understanding between both parties. This approach allows for a more personalized and empathetic interaction, as it provides insight into one's experiences and emotions. By sharing these aspects of their lives, individuals can foster a sense of trust and vulnerability, creating a solid foundation for a meaningful relationship. However, it is important to note that when dealing with a narcissist, this approach can have the opposite effect. Narcissists are known for their self-centeredness and lack of empathy, making it difficult for them to genuinely connect or understand others on a deeper level. In such cases, it may be more effective to focus on setting boundaries and prioritizing self-care, as engaging in discussions about past relationships and traumas may only serve to further enable their manipulative behavior.

I'm Your Secret

In most of these relationships, I was a secret. People didn't know about me. They were so secretive on social media. They claimed they liked privacy, but it was more than that. My son's father and my ex-husband would block posts that they were tagged in on Facebook so their other little girlfriends wouldn't see that they were in a relationship.

My ex-husband claimed all these people from his family knew about me and knew we got married, but I later found out no one knew anything about me or who I was and sure didn't know that he got married. He changed his relationship status on Facebook to married, but he changed the settings so the only person who could see it was me. He requested that I don't change my last name or post pictures of him on social media because if I commented on his page people would know more than they should, but he stuck by his reasoning of wanting this for his privacy. It got to a point that he ended up blocking me on social media because he said he didn't want to hear any more of my bull shit about social media and what is or isn't on his page.

Facebook was where he had a lot of women. His inbox was filled with women from all different states. These women were sending him provocative pictures and telling him the things they would do to him when they saw him. They were pretty upset when I made the post on his Facebook page about having a wife this entire time.

Reality

A man may have valid reasons for not posting about his relationship on social media. However, another reason could be that he wants to keep his relationship status hidden from other women. Pay close attention to his reasons and if they don't sound right, trust your instincts. Privacy and secrecy are two distinct concepts in a relationship. Privacy refers to the personal space and boundaries that individuals maintain, even when in a committed partnership. It allows for autonomy and the ability to have personal thoughts, feelings, and experiences that are not shared with the partner. Secrecy, on the other hand, involves intentionally withholding information or engaging in behaviors that are deceptive and dishonest. It undermines trust and can lead to the erosion of the relationship. Couples need to respect each other's privacy while maintaining open and honest communication. By doing so, they can foster a healthy and trusting relationship based on mutual understanding and respect.

Making Excuses for His Behavior

Throughout my life, I have encountered numerous situations in which I have tolerated behavior that I should never have tolerated. Despite this, I have consistently tried to perceive the good in people and give them the benefit of the doubt. Regrettably, I have often disregarded my intuition, dismissing it as mere paranoia stemming from my fear of being hurt. However, it has become abundantly clear that my intuition has always been accurate in warning me about men who were detrimental to my well-being. I must acknowledge that I allowed myself to be hurt and permitted these men to treat me with less respect than I deserved. I consciously chose to remain in these toxic relationships, despite knowing deep down that it was not in my best interest, and that it would only hurt me more the longer I stayed. They were completely indifferent to my departure, whether it be at the beginning of our relationship or on any subsequent day, as they never harbored any concern for my well-being. Their love for me was nonexistent, yet I remained captivated by their potential or the facade they presented until their true nature was revealed. I clung to the hope that the person I had fallen in love with would resurface. I persisted in the belief that if I complied with their every desire, they would finally treat me with the respect and kindness I deserved. Alas, this scenario never materialized. Although they briefly showered me with adoration for a few days, perhaps a week or two, placing me on a pedestal and feigning importance, it swiftly reverted to degrading behavior, name-calling, and the incessant undermining of my self-worth.

These fleeting moments of benevolence were short-lived. I made numerous excuses for the way he treated me, rationalizing his behavior with thoughts like "he was just having a bad day" or "if I had done what he asked, he wouldn't have hit me". I even convinced myself that if I had apologized sooner, he wouldn't have called me worthless, but the truth is, there is no justification for him to belittle me or make me feel unworthy of love and respect. By allowing these men to control my happiness, I lost myself and despised the person I saw in the mirror. The cruel words spoken by someone I believed loved me were beyond comprehension.

I found myself in the position of having to pick up the shattered fragments of a situation that had gone awry. Despite my better judgment, I chose to remain amid the chaos which ended up only hurting me and hurting me more. No reason or excuse in the world justifies anyone belittling you or making you feel like you are deserving of love and respect. I allowed these men to take away my power and control my happiness and in doing that I lost myself. I hated the person I was in the mirror. I hated everything about me. The mean and hateful things a man that I thought loved me could say were unreal.

Reality

Making excuses for his abusive behavior is not only unacceptable, but it also perpetuates a harmful cycle of violence. Abusive behavior is a serious issue that must be addressed and condemned without reservation. Excusing or justifying such behavior only serves to enable the abuser and further victimize the survivor. We must hold individuals accountable for their actions and provide support and resources to those affected by abuse. By refusing to make excuses for abusive behavior, we can create a society that prioritizes safety, respect, and equality for all. It's time to recognize that no one deserves to be treated this way and reclaim our power. Let us reject any form of abuse and stand up for ourselves, embracing a future filled with self-love and respect.

He Never Loved Me

They have all spoken the words, I love you to me and, at that moment, when they first said it, I believed it and honestly the way my ex-husband made me feel at the beginning, I had never felt before. He could have told me the sun was purple and I would have believed him. I thought to myself, I never knew that being loved could feel this good. Finally, a man who truly loves me. No, it was part of his love bombing. He did and said everything right to sweep me off my feet, fall head over heels for him, and put me exactly where he wanted me, under his control. He conned me. He never loved me. He doesn't know what love is or even how to love.

You Loved the Way I Loved You

In my last relationship, he asked me at the very beginning if I believed in love at first sight and I said that I did. His response was, "When you know, you know." I completely agree with that. I fell so fast for him. Our chemistry was like no other. It was perfect. He was perfect. Before I knew it, I was head over heels with him and loved every minute I spent with him. I told myself repeatedly in my head, I love this man. I love this man. He was the first relationship in five years since leaving my ex-husband. I thought that I would never be able to feel what I felt before, but I was wrong. I felt everything plus more when I was with him.

The first time I attempted to say I love you, I froze. I couldn't get the words to come out. I tried three times before he left my house that day. I even pulled him back towards me when he started to leave, but nothing would come out. I couldn't do it. I texted him as soon as he left and I said, "I tried to say it, but I couldn't". He replied, "Well, I hope I don't die today". Not the response I was expecting or wanted, but I responded with, "I love you, Jay!" He texted me back and said, "I love you, too". My heart melted. I was sure he loved me before he said it because of other non-verbal and indirect signals he had given, but to have him say it was everything.

The honeymoon phase seemed to end quickly, and red flags started to surface, and I chose not to ignore those signs. I started looking into those red flags and low and behold, he is still married and living with his wife and his three children. The same woman he claimed he separated from seven years ago. I felt so dumb! I was crushed! Jay never loved me! He loved the way I loved him. He knew exactly what he was doing and had no regard for how it would make me feel or how I would feel when I discovered the truth. When I ended everything, he didn't fight back. All he said was, "I understand." He knew he was wrong, and he knew everything I said had truth behind it. It still hurt, but I knew I had to let him go, otherwise, I would be heading back down the same path of destruction and heartache. At first, I beat myself up because it felt like I hadn't learned anything over the last five years through my healing journey, but I did! I finally followed my intuition and remembered my worth.

Honestly, I don't think any man has ever truly loved me, but I see now that I didn't love myself either. During my marriage, Camari had multiple women in and out of the door. I'm not sure of the number, but I'm positive it's not the answer I ever wanted to know because it truly disgusts me to think about it. He never loved me. Again, he loved the way I loved him. My undivided attention was on him. He had a place to lay his head, he had money in his pocket and his needs were satisfied any time he wanted whether he wanted food in his stomach, a full body massage, the latest pair of Jordan's, or a sexual desire fulfilled. I never hesitated to make sure he was happy, but it never mattered what I did, because it was never enough. He loved what I did, but he always wanted more. He would manipulate the situation if I told him I didn't have the money for something and guilt. I allowed this man to put me in a financial bind over trying to make him happy.

Reality

Money cannot buy happiness. While materialistic possessions may provide temporary pleasure, they do not guarantee genuine love and affection from others. Love is a complex emotion that cannot be acquired through wealth alone. True happiness and love stem from meaningful connections, shared experiences, and emotional fulfillment. Focus on cultivating genuine relationships and personal growth, as these are the true sources of happiness and love.

If he truly loved you, he would prioritize your feelings and treat you with respect and consistency. Love should never make someone feel like they are just an option or less deserving of care and consideration. It is important to recognize your worth and not settle for anything less than being treated with love and kindness. It is essential to set boundaries and communicate your needs. Remember that you deserve to be with someone who values and cherishes you unconditionally. Trust your instincts and prioritize your well-being.

"You're Not Pretty Enough"

I would go to great lengths to doll myself up, not only to feel pretty but to look pretty to him just to get, "You look alright. My ex Amy looks better than you." Wait a minute!? WHAT? Was that necessary? That was a stab in the heart. I tried so hard to be enough for this man, for him to look at me the same way he viewed this ex of his, but he never treated her right either. She told him, "I hope you beat her ass the same way you used to beat mine since she thinks she's better than everyone because you haven't put your hands on her yet". Why on God's green earth would a woman who has endured his pain and mental, emotional, and physical abuse wish that on another woman? It's disgusting!

I was sick for an unknown reason and lost a lot of weight in a short period of time right before I met him. When we met, I was a size three. I gained some back while I was with him, but it was minimal weight, and I was a size five. I still was too skinny in my opinion, but not to him. I was called fat daily. I was never skinny enough for him. My physical appearance did not meet his standards.

He expressed his dissatisfaction with the size of my buttocks and the attractiveness of my face. I was never allowed to leave the house and be out in public with him without makeup. I always had to have my hair done. Even when I dressed up, he told me I looked OK or decent. He made it very clear that I fell short in every aspect. I found myself questioning why he chose to be with me if he held such negative beliefs about me. Despite the negative influence of this man, I chose to remain in his presence. Over time his demeaning words and actions led me to internalize a belief that I am unattractive and despise my own body, mirroring his sentiments.

Reality

A man who truly loves you would never belittle you or degrade your physical appearance. It is important to recognize that genuine love is built on respect, kindness, and acceptance. When someone truly cares about you, they see your beauty beyond your looks. They appreciate your inner qualities, your personality, and the unique traits that make you who you are. A loving partner understands that beauty is subjective and goes beyond superficial appearances. They uplift you and support you, boosting your self-confidence and making you feel cherished. Remember, you deserve to be with someone who values and appreciates you for who you are, inside and out.

Remind yourself every day that you are undeniably attractive and capable. Your physical appearance meets the standards of beauty, and your abilities and qualities are more than sufficient. It is a fact that you possess the necessary qualities to succeed and excel in various areas of your life. Look at how far you have come. You should embrace this truth and have confidence in your worth. Believe in yourself and recognize your potential. With your inherited qualities, you can achieve great things and make a positive impact. It is critical to recognize the harm that such toxic individuals can inflict upon your esteem and mental well-being. You can transform into a person that you no longer recognize. By consciously rejecting their negative influence and seeking support from positive sources, we can begin to rebuild our self-confidence and embrace our bodies with love and acceptance.

Crying Myself to Sleep

Countless nights I cried myself to sleep, and they never cared. It was their gaslighting and blame-shifting that made me feel like I was inadequate and everything I did was never enough to make them happy. I was never enough for them.

My ex-husband was known to intentionally start a fight right before bed, give me the silent treatment, and then roll over and go to sleep. It was like he found joy in the hurt that he caused me. It didn't affect him at all. Then the next day he would act like nothing ever happened making it seem like I was crazy because I was still upset about the previous night and because he had "moved on" from it, what I was feeling didn't matter so he didn't see the need to talk about it, at least until the next argument and he would throw it in my face again.

Reality

A man who truly loves you will always ensure that the woman he is with never goes to bed angry or upset. This is a crucial aspect of a healthy and harmonious relationship. By addressing any issues or conflicts before bedtime, he demonstrates his commitment to resolving problems and maintaining emotional well-being. This approach fosters open communication, trust, and mutual respect between partners. It is a powerful way to cultivate a strong and lasting bond.

"That Never Happened"

My Exes never took accountability for their actions. They were always the victims and always had a justification for what happened or were deflecting everything thing that took place. Making it seem like I misconstrued the events that happened or just made them up in my head.

My son's father still to this day likes to say that I made up lies in court to get a protection from abuse order against him by telling stories that never happened. How can you deny physical evidence from an event? Between physical abuse and verbal abuse in text messages, there is plenty of evidence to go off for me to get the protection order approved. An incident he denies happened. I remember it like it was yesterday. It was 5:15 a.m. on a workday and he and I were in the car on our way for me to drop him off at his house before I went to work. He wanted to take my car while I was working, and I told him no because the last time he got my car towed for parking in a no-parking zone, he left me stranded at work and I had to fend for myself to get my car out of the tow yard. He was irate that I told him no. He called me by every name in the book. Even started saying how I was going to be a horrible mother and he was the only one that knew anything about being a parent. At one point he punched my rearview mirror because he was angry. I wouldn't budge on him taking my car. At that point, I was scared he was going to punch me while I was driving down the highway. We continued arguing and then he said, "Don't think I won't grab this steering wheel and run us into the back of that truck and kill all of us". Inside I was panicking. What do I do? I see the truck parked alongside the highway, but where am I supposed to stop? My thoughts were a mess. Luckily the truck exited the highway before we got close to it. I was in the clear at that moment.

We exited the highway. He was still telling me how horrible of a mother I was going to be and kept calling our son "that baby". We were about a mile from his house when he grabbed the gear shift and slammed my car into park as I was still driving. I told him to get out of the car. I was done. I couldn't do it anymore. He could walk the rest of the way. I didn't care at that point that there were eight inches of snow on the ground, and it was freezing. He had to go. He said, "Make me". I went to grab my phone and he took it out of my hands and threw it out of the car into the street. When I went to get it, he finally got out of the car. When I tried to get back into my car, he blocked me from getting in. Then he said "Okay, you want me to go. I got it." He grabbed my purse out of the car and started walking up the street with it and throwing it on the snowbank. I retrieved my belongings from the snowbank, and he continued his walk to his house. I was an emotional wreck on my way to work. I even left work early that day, but according to him this event never even took place.

My ex-husband would call me crazy when I talked about things that he did because he completely denied it ever happening. When giving specifics about what occurred, he would continue to deny it. He would tell me I needed to go get help because I was imagining things.

They were both very good at shifting the blame on me to make it look like I was crazy or delusional. They were always the victims of any of our altercations.

Reality

When a man uses the phrase "that never happened," he is attempting to manipulate your mind by gaslighting you. Gaslighting is a form of psychological manipulation where the manipulator seeks to make the victim doubt their reality. By denying the occurrence of an event that you clearly remember, the manipulator aims to make you question your sanity and perception of reality. This tactic is often used in abusive relationships or by individuals with a desire to control and dominate others. It is important to recognize this manipulative behavior and not allow yourself to be swayed by it. Trust your own experiences and instincts, and seek support from trusted friends, family, or professionals if you find yourself in a situation where gaslighting is occurring. By being aware of this manipulation tactic, you can protect your mental well-being and assert your reality.

Black and Blue

I've been strangled to the point of blacking out. I've been beaten until I bled and then told, "If you hadn't done that, I wouldn't have hit you" or "You made me do it". I would coward down and apologize a lot of times in hopes I wouldn't be hit again. My neighbors called the cops numerous times during arguments, and I specifically remember the one time I had blood all over my hands and he told me to go clean myself up and come back out here and act like you have some sense. When I came out of the bathroom, I tucked my hands into my sleeves. Two officers were standing in my living room and asked me if everything was alright. I shook my head yes and said I was fine, but I wasn't fine. I was hurt and I was scared, but I was more scared of my boyfriend retaliating if I told the police what had happened.

Another time he became physically violent was after we were arguing, and he was giving me the silent treatment and I asked him to talk to me. I was standing in front of him, but not aggressively and he grabbed me by my throat and choked me until I blacked out. When I came to, it took me a minute to remember what had just happened. I saw him in the closet throwing stuff around and I remember thinking I have to get out of here. I got up from the bed and started running towards the door. He came running after me, grabbed me by my ponytail, and threw me onto the couch. He then grabbed me by my feet and dragged me off the couch. On the way down to the floor, he hit my head on the bamboo frame of the couch. He proceeded to crawl on top of me and grabbed me by my throat and said, "Bitch, I'm going to fuckin' kill you". After a couple of seconds, I started going into convulsions and was struggling to breathe and he got scared. A few seconds longer, I'm sure I would have been dead. He stopped choking me and started to console me. I was trying to tell him to get off me, get off me, but I was so weak. He picked me up, carried me to the bathroom, and put me in the tub. He turned on the water to run a bath and kept telling me he was sorry and that everything was going to be okay.

Unfortunately, that wasn't the last time he put his hands on me. We had gone on a cruise together and his cousin came along. I paid for all of us to go on this trip. That was supposed to be a stress-free time full of fun. Instead, he left me in our room for hours by myself and when he and his cousin returned, I was visibly upset and asked him where they had been. He never liked being questioned about things that he did, and he made it about him and tried to leave me in the room again saying he wasn't going to deal with this shit. I asked him to come back and grabbed his hand. He punched me in the face dislocating my jaw and then right after that he pushed me through an automatic closing door which ended up closing on my legs. Staff intervened and I was carried down to the emergency room on the ship to be evaluated. The next day there was going to be an emergency hearing and they were going to force him to get off at the next port. They gave us separate rooms for the night. Jason talked me into going to his room to talk and his goal was to talk me out of telling them what happened, so he didn't kick him off the ship. I complied and told them that we were both drunk and we got a little out of hand and asked them to let him stay for the remainder of the cruise. I lied to protect him and to make him happy, yet I was still hurting and broken inside, and he didn't care. He was only worried about himself. That wasn't the vacation we were supposed to have, but I should have expected it to go badly seeing as his patterns of abuse are consistent.

My son's father started by only being verbally and emotionally abusive, but it escalated very quickly. He constantly belittled me and called me names. He broke a candle once during an argument because he threw it. The next thing I knew, there was blood everywhere and it was my fault because I made him throw the candle. After we got the mess cleaned up, I told him he needed to leave. He refused to go. He put his head in his duffle bag and said, "Bitch, I got my gun". He told me he wasn't scared to shoot me. At that time, I didn't know if his gun was in his bag or not. I grabbed my phone, and he came after me, took my phone, and threw it across the room. He then proceeded to take the PS5, which I was still paying for, and I told him "No, that isn't yours, it's mine." I was around three months pregnant at the time of this incident and he jammed the PS5 into my stomach and said, "I hope you die along with that baby". We ended up tussling after that and I finally broke myself free and found my phone and called 911. While on the phone with the dispatcher he grabbed me by my ponytail and yanked my head back so hard that I got whiplash from it. By the time the police arrived he had already taken off on foot. EMS evaluated me and the baby and everything was fine. I ended up filing for protection from abuse and it was granted for three years. I moved 600 miles away to go into hiding. I knew for at least three years, my son and I would be safe.

Reality

It is an absolute fact that a man who truly loves you would never, under any circumstances, physically harm you. This is a non-negotiable aspect of a healthy and loving relationship. You must recognize and understand this truth. If you find yourself in a situation where you are being physically hurt by a man who claims to love you, you must take immediate action to remove yourself from that harmful environment. Your safety and well-being should always be your top priority. Seek support from trusted friends, family, or professionals who can assist you in navigating this difficult situation. Remember, you deserve to be treated with respect, kindness, and love at all times.

Part Two

The Relationships in a Nutshell

My Son's Father

He had a lot of women, but that explains why he was so jealous and insecure. I tried getting back into music while we were together. I had a studio in my house, and I had finished writing and recording a song that I originally started writing about two years previously. When he heard the song he automatically accused me of wanting to be with an ex and started a huge argument over it, when all I wanted to do was finish what I started. I wasn't thinking about anyone while finishing it, but he wasn't hearing that. I also scheduled to meet with a music producer, and it took too long for Leroy's liking and I got accused of going there to sleep with the guy instead of going for what I said I was going for. He blew my phone up while I was there, but I was in a meeting with the producer discussing what things would look like if I moved forward. I ended up giving up my music dream because I couldn't deal with all the accusations. It was too much.

Leroy was verbally and physically abusive. His verbal abuse was the worst. Any opportunity he got to tear me down, he would. He belittled me and called me names constantly. He made me feel worthless and inadequate most days like I could never do anything right. He was the main one who denied events ever happening. He denies the incident in the car about threatening to kill us and putting my car in park while I was driving. He denies ever assaulting me and trying to kill our son while I was pregnant. Everything also came down to race with him. He always made comments that started like, "Oh because I'm black...", or "Oh because you're white. You white people are cop callers." To this day he likes to call me a cop caller because I called the police to protect myself and my child from his abuse. He's mad at me because he went to jail, but it's because of his actions, but he takes no responsibility.

Even though I haven't seen him since I was six months pregnant with our son, I still deal with his abuse. I have chosen not to respond anymore. Blocking him doesn't stop him because he uses text now numbers and creates a new number every time he texts me or tries to call me blocked, but I never answer blocked calls, because I already assume it is him. He blames me for not being a part of his son's life, but again, that is his own doing. I have tried countless times to have him meet his son and become an active father, but he wants to try to control and dictate how things are going to go. No, this is not how it works. I have been the one raising our son, providing everything he needs without a penny or a thought from you so you aren't going to tell me how we are doing things. He says I'm just bitter. I'm not bitter and I'm not angry. I'm taking care of and protecting our son from anything that is toxic to him and you being in and out, disappearing for six months at a time then randomly texting me after you blow him off doesn't fly with me. It's all in or all out. Pick one. Last time I told him that he said "All out. Not like I know him. I don't want to deal with you anyway." Trying to co-parent with a narcissist is not easy, because he tries to counter-parent. I just shut him down and told him at this point if he wants to see his son contact the courts because they are looking for him for two child support; for his son and his daughter with another woman.

Ex-Husband

He is Satan himself. Our relationship started with multiple lies. He said he had three children, and they were with his first ex-wife. Our daughter together is number 12 which we know of. He got another woman pregnant while I was pregnant. Our daughter has a sister three months younger than her. He now has 14 or 15 kids, but we don't know because he lives his life in secret. He claims he likes privacy. The man uses different aliases because he knows that as soon as you google his government name, his mug shots pop up. He doesn't want his new supply to know the kind of monster he is before he can put them under his control and make everyone else seem like they have it out for him.

When we first met, he said his biological mother and sister both passed away and he had to pay for both funerals by himself because the rest of the family wouldn't help. I came to find out that both his mother and sister were alive when we met, and it wasn't until after we got married that his sister passed away from breast cancer. I asked him if that was the same sister he had said passed away before we met, and he said yes then changed the subject. His mother was still alive, just not an active part of his life. When asked about lying about his mother being dead, he said, "She's dead to me" but he said he paid for the funerals.

There were so many women. I had women messaging me on Facebook about him and he would tell me to block them and that they were just jealous. A woman even sent screenshots of a text conversation between the two of them and he said that they were fake and not to entertain her. Just to block her. His saying to block her was the easiest way for him to avoid anyone ever knowing the truth about the things he was doing.

Camari would intentionally set things up and watch them spiral out of control. One day I was at work and he was home. It was about 20 minutes before I was leaving work on a Monday, and he sent me a text message with a picture. It said, "I found this while I was cleaning the house. Would you care to explain? Don't text me back either, or wait until you get home. Call me". The picture he attached was of him holding up a condom with a pen. All I could think about was, are you serious right now? At the same time, I wasn't shocked by this coming from him. I knew that wasn't from me and I already knew he was up to one of his mind games. Before I could reply or call him, he sent another text stating, "And before you say I planted it, I didn't". And there you have it. He already called himself out. He knew what he was doing. I called and said I don't know where it came from because it wasn't me". When I arrived, he started asking me a million questions and I told him the same thing I did on the phone, it's not from me. I didn't cheat on you. He finally dropped it and said, "I'm horny. Let's go have sex." Wait a minute, you just tried to set me up and accuse me of sleeping with someone else and now you want to have sex? If it were me who found the condom, I would be completely disgusted at the thought of sleeping with him. I mean I was already feeling that way because he planned all this out in his sick mind for whatever reason, but it didn't go as he had planned.

Another time he set me up it took me some time to put the pieces together to realize it was him. He played the part of a caring husband at the time though. It was on a weekend, and I was in the kitchen making breakfast and my ex-husband was upstairs. Just as breakfast was about to be ready, my phone went off with a text message. It read, "I wanna fuck!" I didn't recognize the number, so I ignored it. I called my ex-husband to come down for breakfast. As he is walking down the stairs, my phone goes off again. I didn't even look at my phone as I was setting up the table. My ex continues to watch something on his phone as he eats.

My phone went off again and he looked up as I picked up my phone and said, "Miss Popular, who's that?" I said I didn't know. He said, "Clearly they know you". He walked back upstairs after he was done eating and my phone went off again. I replied, "I don't know who this is, but I'm not interested. I'm in a relationship".

Immediately after I received a hateful text stating, "Bitch, you don't know who this is but yet you carried my child? I wanna know how my daughter is. You're white trash. Your man doesn't even love you. He's only with you because you're easy." My oldest daughter's father has never spoken to me like that. He never called me names, never swore at me and now I'm getting texts degrading me...Something isn't right.

The messages stopped for the rest of the day, but I did end up telling my ex-husband about the messages and showing him and he said if they text you again, let me know. The next day, as soon as I got to work, another text came from the same number. I called my ex-husband and told him they had texted me again. He asked me to send him the number so he could call. He stated he tried to call but there was no answer. He acted all upset that my daughter's father was creating all this drama for nothing, and it was out of the blue after hearing nothing from him.

I ended up calling the number that I had for my daughter's father, and he answered. I proceeded to tell him I didn't appreciate his uncalled-for text messages and that he needed to leave me alone. He had no idea what I was talking about. He even asked me, "Have I ever spoken to you like that?"

"Well, no! No, you haven't, but you aren't who I thought you were anyway, so nothing would surprise me at this point." After that, I heard nothing else from that random number that texted me.

Fast forward to the conversation that my ex and I had about his grandmother, whom he called "mom". He always told me that his mother hated me, but yet she had never met me, and I never did anything to this woman. He would tell me things that she said about me, and our relationship and it would make me so angry. Why does this woman hate me so much? He would tell me the names she would call me and the awful things she would say, and it would piss me off further. He also told me that his best friend, whom he had dated years previous, hated me as well. Again, I had never met or talked to this girl. Why? And why is he allowing this woman to bad mouth me and you are okay with it?

Finally, one day, he slipped up when telling me about things his mom and his best friend had said about me. They called me white trash, a whore, and a few other derogatory things that triggered my memory. It was as soon as he said that, I remembered the text messages. That was it, it was his mom and or his best friend because they hate me and have been trying to get rid of me. So, I said to my ex-husband, "I know it wasn't Felix that sent me those text messages". He responded with, "I thought you said you didn't know who it was?"

"I didn't, but I do now. It was either your mom or Dana."

The look in this man's eyes when I accused them of doing this scared the shit out of me. I had never seen that look before and I knew it wasn't going to end well. He snapped and started yelling and screaming at me and said "Don't ever blame them for anything again". He was all up in my face. "See this is why they don't like your ass because you are always doing dumb shit. They will want to fuck you up when they hear about this. Give me one good reason why I shouldn't pack my stuff and leave now?" I told him that I had messaged Felix and he said it wasn't him and that he had no idea what I was talking about. Then he started yelling again because I reached out to Felix and didn't tell him and the fact that I believed Felix when he said he didn't do it. I ended up cowering down to him just to calm the situation, but I still knew something wasn't right about the whole texting situation.

Months had gone by since the incident and I still wasn't sure exactly who sent those texts until a fight that we got into, and he said numerous things that were in those text messages. That's when I realized it was him the whole time. Who does that? He caused so many issues, for what? To this day, I don't understand the purpose of what he did, but one thing I did learn after I left him, is that he did similar things to other girlfriends in previous relationships. He had a man arrested for stalking, even though it was he who did it. The woman got scared because she thought it was the guy she had dated last. That charge will forever be on that man's record now, because of the things my ex-husband did.

He made me believe that everyone in his family hated me and would tell me often that his mom would tell him every time they talked that he needed to divorce me. Sometimes he would act like he was so angry with his mom about her saying things about me and said that he had to defend me because she didn't stop going in about me. What I learned is, that when he did stuff like that, he did get into a heated argument or altercation with someone, but it wasn't with who he said, nor did it have anything to do with me.

Camari said he went to a friend's house to visit then called me pretty late at night angry stating that he and his friend's wife got into a yelling match and went off on a tangent about how he can't stand her and that he was going to have to stay in his car because it was too late for him to drive back home. I asked him where the closest hotel was and made a reservation for him for the night. He was still talking about the event that had happened and was fuming. I told him to rest and talk to his friend in the morning.

Two days had passed, and Camari had just left the house for work. He called me shortly after he left the house in a panic and asked, "Did you call the cops on me?" I was so confused. He just left the house. What is he talking about? He said, "The police are arresting me, and they won't tell me why. Are you sure you didn't call the police?" I said, "Yes, I'm sure. What the hell is going on?

Can I talk to one of the officers?" One of the officers got on the phone and stated that he had a warrant for his arrest and that I could call the jail shortly to get his booking information. I was so confused as to what was going on, but I eventually talked to someone at the jail, and they told me he had been arrested for strangulation, armed robbery, criminal confinement, pointing a firearm at another, domestic battery, and domestic battery in the presence of a child less than 16. That was a lot to take in. I had never known him to be this person.

I messaged his friend that he said he was with the other night to find out what happened that night with his wife. His friend called me and I demanded to know what happened that night. He said, "I don't know. I don't want to get involved in this." I said, "Dan, I need to know what happened." He then proceeded to tell me that Camari was never at his house. He went to another woman's house to get the rest of his stuff from there and things went left. He tried to back it up with, Camari does love you and that's why he was getting his stuff. I asked Dan who he was living with when I first met Camari and asked if he ever stayed with him since that is what Camari told me. Again, he tried to deflect and say he didn't want to get involved but it was too late. Camari never lived with Dan or the other two friends he claimed he stayed with. Dan named three different women that Camari was staying with, one of whom he caught all of those charges. And here my dumbass was believing him about getting into an argument with his friend's wife and I put him up in a hotel.

I also messaged his mom on Facebook to let her know what was going on and to please call me. I even stated I know you don't like me, but I don't know what else to do. When she called me she said she had no idea who I was and didn't believe that Camari and I were married. So, I broke everything down as to who I was, when we got married, and the things he told me she said about me. She cleared the air and one thing that stood out to me in that conversation with her was her saying, "A leopard never changes its spots. Leave and leave now." I should have listened to her back then.

Once he was done booking and able to call me I again asked him what had happened. He still acted like I had no idea what was going on and I informed him of what the jail told me. He finally said, "I was at the girl's house to get my stuff out and she became upset because I didn't want to be with her, and she found out about you and I getting married, and she pulled her gun on me. I had to take the gun from her because she was going to shoot me."

Here I am again, believing this crazy story because I didn't know him to be violent like this. Then I decided to Google his name. I should have done that from the very beginning and avoided all of this, but lesson learned. The first thing I see is a mugshot of him with the caption of him admitting to impersonating a police officer. What? This is crazy. I started piecing more of his fabricated stories together. Every story he ever told had some kind of truth behind it, but he was never at fault in his stories.

When we met he was on probation, and he told me the reason he was on probation was because he saw a man putting his hands on a woman and that wasn't something he condoned. So he went and helped the woman and hit the man, but it was a very different story that happened. He was the one who was going after a woman and pulling her over by impersonating a police officer. It was after that that all of his skeletons started coming out of the closet. Now I'm seeing this man for who he is. A monster. A risk and danger to my health and well-being. I have to get out before I get into an even worse situation.

While he was in jail, I accessed his Facebook account. Now I don't necessarily condone this, but I wanted answers. That's when I found at least a dozen women just from conversations in his inbox.

No one could see that he was in a relationship or married because I was a secret from everyone. I was livid after all that I had done for this man, and this is how I'm treated.

I posted a picture of me and him with a caption that said,

"This is my beautiful wife. Yes, my wife and because I couldn't keep my dick in my pants, I lost the best thing that has ever happened to me. That made even more women come out of the woodwork. They sent private messages like "How could you and you were married?" "I hate you!" Just a lot of angry women in his inbox.

This is how his family found out about me. All his sisters and female cousins were reaching out to me, and I started to build a relationship with them, they told me a lot of deep dark secrets that Camari hid from me throughout our entire relationship. That is when I found out his birth mother was still alive and well. I found out about more children (but not all of them at that time). It wasn't until another mother of two of his children reached out to me when I was living in the domestic violence shelter and told me about all the other children and the shit storm that he put her through. All too similar to what I was going through with him. Ten years later, he is still doing the same thing just different women.

He always keeps at least three women on hand. He has the one he's living with, one that is there and ready for him to move in but he's giving excuses to hold her off until the current live-in girlfriend is sick of his shit and kicks him out then he has a new place to lay his head at night and the third girlfriend is just out on a whim and he's giving her enough attention to keep her interested but not too much just in case a better option might come along or at least until she is in the second spot, then he will pour it on hard. He needs a woman to survive because he can't get a decent job or keep a job for that matter which means he doesn't have the money to be able to pay for a house. He uses women for everything they have and once they either run out of money or see through his bull shit, he kicks them to the curb, but he is already a step ahead and halfway moved in with his next supply, so he isn't homeless.

My First Love

When we first met, everything was perfect. He lived 280 miles away from me. Every weekend for four months, I made that four-and-a-half-hour drive to see him, or he came to me. Then my father threw me out for dating a black man and I told Jason that he either needed to move here or we would have to break up because I couldn't afford to make that drive anymore. So that's what he did. He packed his stuff and we moved into our apartment together. The first nine months of our relationship were perfect. I knew about his past and his history of domestic violence, but that was never an issue. We never fought. We never argued. It was everything I could have wanted it to be, but then one day, he completely changed, and the person I once knew and fell in love with no longer existed. I tried to hold on to the person he was, but he was never real. That's who he wanted me to see, who he wanted me to fall in love with. It's love bombing. He had a hold on me like no one else had.

After this new version of him surfaced, I could never do anything right. We fought and argued about everything. I was accused of cheating on him if I arrived home ten minutes later from work than I normally did. I tried to free myself from him so many times, but I always went back because I couldn't let go of the person I fell in love with. This man almost killed me twice. Why couldn't I let him go? I was so brainwashed and completely lost who I was and my self-worth. I love him with every fiber of my being, but I couldn't understand why he couldn't see that and why he treated me the way that he did.

One of the last times that I ended things, he kept trying to smooth everything over, but I stood my ground even though I wanted nothing more than to hug him. It hurt so badly, but I knew I needed to let go. He eventually hopped on his motorcycle and left.

A week later he called and said I want you to drive out here and show me how much you love me. My response was, "I've shown you how much I love you over the past two years, it's your turn". He didn't like the response and hung up on me.

The next day when I arrived home from work, he was sitting in the driveway at my house. I asked him what he was doing here, and he said he wanted to go in and talk. I told him no, that we could stay outside, and he could tell me what he needed to say. Of course, it was everything I wanted to hear. I told him he had two weeks for me to see a change or he was going to be right back out the door. A week later, he went back home to celebrate his cousin's birthday. One night I was leaving work and I called him. He was out at the bar and there was a lot of noise in the back-ground so I was yelling so he could hear me. He said, "Who the fuck are you talking to?" I said, "I'm not yelling at you. I'm yelling so you can hear me." Well, that didn't fly with him. He proceeded to yell at me demanding I apologize to him. I told him I wasn't going to apologize because I didn't do anything wrong. The last thing I said to him was, "This is why we will never work out and why we can't be together". The last thing he said to me was, "Fuck you, Bitch" and he hung up. I heard nothing else from him for the rest of the night.

The next morning around 10 a.m., I received a text message from his cousin that said, "Jason was in an accident. I'm so scared!" I called his cousin to get more details. He had left the bar drunk after our argument, got into his car, and got into an accident. I dropped everything I was doing and headed out to Pittsburgh to the hospital. It was so bad, and I kept replaying our conversation over and over in my head. I didn't mean for that to be the last thing that I said to him, but I couldn't take it back. I meant it because I didn't deserve all the mental, emotional, and physical abuse, but damn...why did this have to happen? They say that things happen for a reason, and I truly believe that this was God's way of saving me, because I think he would have ended up killing me. I loved that man and would have done anything for him, but he was so bad for me. Sometimes love just isn't enough.

Our relationship started with a lie. He neglected to tell me that he was still married and still living with her. After doing my research, I found documents showing he was married but still claiming they are separated just living together for the past seven years as roommates and he sleeps in a different bed/room. When he is at home, his phone is always on do not disturb me and if he calls me, he is always in his truck. He said the reason he couldn't talk at the house was because his kids didn't need to hear the conversation. Well, what is it we are talking about that isn't appropriate for your kids, but it's appropriate for mine? No, your wife is the reason!

He was probably the most jealous and insecure person that I have ever dealt with. It was a lot and very exhausting. He would grill me about any man that I ever brought up, was around Facebook friends, Snapchat, you name it. He got very jealous when I told him I was braiding my neighbor's hair. He started asking a million questions and saying, "Well doesn't he like you? Does he flirt with you? Has anything ever happened to you guys?

No, damn! Back off. I'm just braiding his hair. I told him when we first met, I braided his hair. Why is it an issue now? He proceeds to say, "I can't compete with your neighbor and braiding". I think that's a bit dramatic. I didn't know that it was a competition. He would get mad because he was texting me while I was braiding and I wouldn't respond right away, but I couldn't. Again, I was braiding someone's hair. He asked for a picture when it was done. I'm sure that was to make sure I did do his hair. That was my first red flag from him because I still hadn't found out about his wife yet.

I used to always post different pictures on my Snapchat story whether it was of my kids or me. I don't dress up often but when I do, I take pictures and post them. I feel good about myself. One day, he unfriended me on Snapchat out of nowhere. I noticed it when I went to snap him a little later and I asked him about it and he said, "I can't handle seeing you posting sexy pictures of yourself, so I did it to protect myself". I don't understand why he felt like he couldn't talk to me about it. To make him more secure, I stopped posting selfies.

Next thing I know my Tik-Toks are an issue. Mind you I haven't created a Tik-Tok in forever. Then he's asking how many Facebook friends I have and how many of the people I talk to on a day-to-day basis have a crush on me or I've ever been intimate with. All of this was just so much for me when I'd done nothing but prove and show, my eyes were all on him. He was all I wanted.

He questioned me about how many friends I had on Facebook and asked how many men and did anything ever happened or if they liked me or flirted with me. So, to try to make him feel more secure, I deleted over 2,000 people from my social media, but it didn't matter because he was going to be insecure either way.

It even got as bad as him stalking me through my Snapchat location. He asked me where I stopped on the way home from my parents. I said, "Nowhere. I came straight home." He said, "Well your Snap location showed you stopped somewhere."

"Yeah! At the stop lights!..."

He noticed almost immediately when I turned my location off and asked me if I was doing something I didn't want him to know about. I just wanted to see how closely he followed me. It was scary.

He obsessed and stalked my snap count number. Apparently, I had told him I was going to bed, but he saw my snap count go up by ten so he snapped me asking, "Who did you snap?" I had no idea what he was talking about because I didn't snap anyone. I said, "What are you talking about?"

He took a screenshot of my snap count and said, "It was this but now it's this. Who were you snapping?" So, I screenshotted my snap list and explained who everyone was that he saw in the screenshot, and I even screenshotted a snap that came in from my cousin and said, "This is the last snap I received." This shit is crazy. Why am I doing this?

I wasn't supposed to talk to anyone I had previous relations with or anyone who liked me, but he refused to cut off two women he was recently sexually involved with. His excuse was, "They have been with me through the thick of it for the past six years" but here I am doing all this, and I'm supposed to cut everyone off? He loved having his double standards for many different things. Oh, you can have a secret wife at home, but you want to become enraged and jealous over me braiding someone's hair, who I've braided before and have never had anything physical with? He knew what he was doing was wrong, but he wanted to make sure I wasn't the one doing the same shit he was doing because he was too worried about protecting himself and that big-ass ego of his.

Part Three

Motivational Quotes:

REMINDING YOURSELF WHAT YOU DESERVE

Begging for the Bare Minimum

I f you find yourself in a situation where you have to beg for the bare minimum from someone, it is clear that he is not the right person for you. It is important to recognize your worth and not settle for anything less than what you deserve. Begging for basic needs or minimal attention is not a healthy or fulfilling relationship dynamic. You deserve to be with someone who values and respects you, someone who willingly provides for your needs and treats you with kindness and consideration. It is crucial to have high standards and not settle for less than you deserve. Remember, you deserve the best and there is someone out there who will meet your needs without you having to beg for it.

Cease All Contact

Cease all attempts to make contact and observe the outcome. By refraining from reaching out, you will be able to assess the response, or lack thereof, from the other party. This approach allows for a clearer understanding of the dynamics at play and provides an opportunity to evaluate the level of interest or engagement of the individual in question. It is important to note that this method has been proven effective in numerous scenarios, as it allows for a more accurate assessment of the situation. Rest assured, by adopting this approach, you are positioning yourself in a favorable position to gauge the true level of interest and determine the next course of action accordingly.

If He Missed You

If he missed you, he would call. It is highly unlikely that someone would be too busy to reach out if they truly cared. Additionally, if you were truly important to him, he would have made that abundantly clear through his actions and words. It is important to recognize and prioritize relationships where both parties feel valued and appreciated. A relationship doesn't work one-sided. Cut your losses! He's not the one!

Believe in Yourself

You matter! Your existence is significant and valuable. Your actions have an impact on the world around you. Embrace your worth and recognize the power you possess. Believe in yourself and your abilities. Take charge of your life and make a difference. Spread positivity and inspire others with your presence. Remember, you are important, and your contributions are essential. Keep shining brightly and never forget the significance of your existence.

Heal Yourself First

When consistently attracting partners who are not interested in a serious commitment, it may be due to your reluctance to commit. This reluctance often stems from a fear of experiencing another heartbreak, particularly if the process of healing from previous heartbreaks was challenging. It is important to acknowledge and address this fear to move towards a healthier and more fulfilling romantic life. By taking the necessary steps to heal and build emotional resilience, you can gradually overcome your fear of commitment and open yourself up to the possibility of a deep and meaningful connection.

I Lost Interest Fast

When it comes to my level of interest, I am not one to "lose interest fast." Rather, I possess the ability to quickly discern whether a situation is progressing or not. I am not hesitant to make necessary changes, as I am fully aware of the value of my time. Just as my interest can peak rapidly, it can also plummet just as swiftly. However, I have no qualms about accepting this change. What was once enjoyable is now recognized as a temporary experience, not something meant to last indefinitely. I hold no ill feelings and have instead learned to appreciate the beauty of new beginnings.

Accepting All of Me

To find someone who loves, appreciates, and accepts you for who you are, it is important to actively seek out individuals who exhibit these qualities. Look for individuals who consistently demonstrate kindness, understanding, and respect for you. Seek out those who actively listen to you, value your opinions, and support your goals and aspirations. Surround yourself with people who celebrate your successes and are there for you during challenging times. Engage in open and honest communication with potential partners, friends, or family members, ensuring that they understand and accept your true self. By actively seeking out individuals who possess these qualities, you increase your chances of finding someone who genuinely loves, appreciates, and accepts you for who you are.

Trust Yourself

Trust your intuition. If your gut says something is off, let it go! Your intuition is a powerful tool that can guide you in making decisions. Research has shown that our gut feelings are often based on the subconscious processing of information and can provide valuable insights. When something feels off, it could be a warning sign that something is not right. By trusting your intuition and letting go of situations that do not align with your instincts, you are taking a proactive approach to protect yourself and make better choices. This can lead to a more fulfilling and successful life. So, embrace your intuition and have confidence in your ability to discern what feels right. Trust your gut and let go of anything that does not pass the intuitive test. You have the power to make wise decisions and create a positive future.

I Choose Me

Choosing oneself above all else is a decision that should be embraced. By prioritizing our own needs and desires, we can cultivate self-care and personal growth. This choice allows us to set boundaries, pursue our passions, and make decisions that align with our values. By making ourselves a priority, we are better equipped to contribute positively to our relationships and communities. It is important to remember that self-care is not selfish, but rather an essential aspect of maintaining overall well-being. Embracing this mindset can lead to increased self-confidence, improved mental and physical health, and a greater sense of fulfillment in life. So, choose yourself above all and watch as your life flourishes.

Cheating

I f your partner cheats, it is advisable to forgive (for yourself), but it is important not to hold on. It is best to walk away from a relationship. This is because when someone cheats, it indicates a lack of remorse for their actions. They are not sorry for cheating, but rather sorry that they were caught. It is crucial to prioritize your well-being and not remain in a relationship where trust has been broken. By moving on, you are allowing yourself to find a partner who will be faithful and committed. Remember, you deserve better.

Cheating in a relationship is an action that should not be given a second chance. It is a breach of trust and a violation of the commitment made to one another. The act of cheating undermines the foundation of a relationship, causing significant emotional pain and damage. Trust is a fundamental element in any healthy relationship, and once it is broken, it becomes difficult to rebuild. By not allowing cheating to be excused or forgiven (and stayed), individuals can maintain their self-respect and protect themselves from further harm. It is important to prioritize one's well-being and seek out relationships built on trust and loyalty.

Red Flags

In any relationship, it is crucial to be aware of red flags that may indicate potential problems. These warning signs should not be ignored, as they can be indicative of deeper issues. One red flag to watch out for is a lack of communication or frequent misunderstandings. Open and honest communication is the foundation of a healthy relationship, so if this is lacking, it may be a cause for concern. Another red flag is controlling behavior or a lack of respect for boundaries. Both partners should have equal say and autonomy in the relationship, and any attempt to control or manipulate the other person is a clear red flag. Additionally, if there is a consistent pattern of dishonesty or betrayal, it is important to address this issue. Trust is essential in a relationship, and repeated instances of lying or cheating can erode that trust. Finally, if there is a lack of support or emotional availability from one partner, it can be detrimental to the relationship. Both individuals should feel supported and valued by their partner. In conclusion, it is vital to pay attention to these red flags and address them early on to maintain a healthy and fulfilling relationship.

Feeling Trapped

Sometimes, you may find yourself feeling trapped in an unhealthy relationship. While it is common to attribute this to the manipulation of the wrong partner or various forms of abuse, there are instances where the fault lies within oneself. In these cases, it is often due to holding tightly onto memories of the past, distorting one's perception of present reality. By fixating on what once was, individuals inadvertently confine themselves to a relationship from which their partner has already moved on. This self-imposed imprisonment manifests itself as physical symptoms such as tightness in the chest and sudden anxiety. The cause of this distress, however, is not the partner, but rather one's reluctance to let go of something that no longer exists. It is crucial to recognize this and take the necessary steps to free oneself from this self-imposed captivity.

Healthy Boundaries

Boundaries are often misunderstood. People think you are trying to control them or telling them what to do. The purpose of recognizing boundaries is not to alter others' behavior or persuade them to prioritize different things. Instead, it is about advocating for oneself, irrespective of their response. This approach empowers individuals to assert their needs and assert their worth. By setting boundaries, one can establish healthy relationships and promote personal well-being. It is a powerful tool that encourages self-respect and fosters respect from others. Embracing boundaries is a crucial step toward personal growth and fulfillment.

Embrace Yourself

One of the most profound and enduring regrets that individuals experience in life is the act of conforming to the expectations and desires of others, rather than embracing and embodying their true selves. This regret stems from the recognition that by prioritizing the opinions and wishes of others over their authentic desires and identities, individuals sacrifice their fulfillment and hinder their potential for genuine happiness and self-actualization. The consequences of succumbing to external pressures and conforming to societal norms can manifest in various ways, such as a sense of emptiness, dissatisfaction, and a pervasive feeling of living a life that is not truly one's own. By contrast, embracing one's true self and pursuing a path aligned with one's values, passions, and aspirations offers the potential for profound personal growth, fulfillment, and a genuine sense of purpose.

It is imperative, therefore, to resist the temptation to conform to external expectations and instead prioritize the development and expression of one's authentic self. By doing so, individuals not only honor their own unique identities but also contribute to a more diverse and vibrant society that celebrates individuality and fosters an environment conducive to personal growth and collective progress. Embracing one's true self is a courageous and empowering act that holds the promise of a life lived with integrity, authenticity, and profound personal fulfillment.

Seeing Them for Who They Are

When you start questioning an abuser they become very defensive and angry because you are seeing through them and seeing them for who they are. The grave problem with hidden abuse lies in the manipulation of the target's emotions. The abuser manufactures feelings for the sake of power and control, while the target remains unaware. Gaslighting, manipulation, deflection, isolation, and shifting blame are all tactics an abuser uses to try to gain or regain control. Any time an abuser is not in control, they panic. Their goal is to have you lose control of your emotions and thoughts and will have you second-guessing everything about you; what you do, who you are, and your self-worth. They want to isolate you and make you feel like you cannot live without them, yet you are an emotional wreck being with them because no matter how hard you try or what you do, you will never feel like you are good enough or worthy enough of their love. When it is quite the opposite. They do not know how to love! They never and will never love you. The only thing they care about is protecting themselves and their ego because deep down inside they hate who they are and they hate nothing more when the real them surfaces and they can no longer hide it from their victim. That's when they will leave because again they have to be in control, control of YOU. If they can't "control" you anymore, you're of no use to them. They have already moved on to the next supply before you have fully seen them for who they are. Their only means of survival are through other people. They are like a parasite without a supply they would die. They need you. You do not need them!

Acceptance

Acceptance is the key to resolving your problems. When you are disturbed, it is because you are unable to accept certain aspects of your life. You must find serenity by accepting people, places, things, and situations exactly as they are supposed to be. I firmly believe that nothing happens by mistake in this world. To find happiness, you must fully accept yourself, your situation, and your life on life's terms. You need to focus on changing yourself and your attitudes rather than being overly concerned about what happens in the world around you. I am confident that embracing acceptance will lead to positive transformation.

You are Blessed

You are too blessed and have too much to offer to settle for someone who doesn't see your value. Love yourself enough to save yourself the heartache from a man who could care less if you left today. Love yourself more!

Double Standards

Relationships do not function properly when there are hypocrisies. There is a double standard when a partner approaches you and says, "You can't have friends of the opposite sex, but I'm not cutting off so-and-so and so-and-so because they have been through the thick of it with me for the past six years." So, let me get this straight, you're unwilling to sever ties with two women you've been intimate with pretty recently because you said they've been there for six years throughout difficult times, but I'm meant to cut off and not speak to any man that I was ever romantically involved with, liked me, hit on me, or had a crush on me? Sir, you are very insecure and to me that screams, I know I am going to cheat, but I want to make sure you cannot go find someone better because I know I'm a piece of shit! Do not allow anyone to tell you to do something if they are not willing to do it themselves.

Distance Breeds Doubt

D istance breeds doubt. Whether it is emotional, mental, or physical. Long-distance relationships can be challenging. In every relationship, having open lines of communication is essential, but it is especially important in long-distance relation-ships because, in many cases, this is all you have until your schedule allows you to be together in person. When your partner is not emotionally available to you, it can lead to a rift and frequently results in you becoming resentful of them since they either weren't there for you when you needed them, or they aren't capable of meeting your emotional needs in a relationship.

His Intentions

Do you question his intentions with you?
Are you constantly wondering where you stand in his life?

Let me break it down easily...

He's not the one if you have doubts. When a man genuinely wants you, he will act and speak in a way that makes it obvious that you are what he wants. When there are men in line who are prepared and eager to give you whatever you desire and more, never beg a man for the bare minimum. Your Prince Charming is waiting for you to realize your worth!

<h1 style="text-align:center">One Last Reminder</h1>

It is crucial to always remember that one does not require the presence of a partner to flourish. Furthermore, it is impossible to heal in an environment that has caused harm. Even if arguments and fights are not occurring in the presence of your children, they can still sense the tension within the household. It is imperative that we are loved properly by our partner, and it is equally important for children to witness their mothers being loved in such a way. Prioritizing self-care is essential before we can fulfill our role as mothers. As a mother myself, I am aware that I often place my own needs on the back burner. However, if I am not in a healthy state of mind, my toxicity can negatively impact my children. This may manifest as snapping at them over trivial matters due to other aspects of my life feeling amiss. Having a support system to rely on for venting, taking breaks, or any other means of regaining the necessary mental space is of utmost importance.

Being a mother is a challenging role that often demands superhero-like qualities. However, it is important to acknowledge that no one is perfect, and it can be exhausting to constantly uphold such high expectations. It is perfectly acceptable to let your crown slip occasionally, as long as you have the determination to pick yourself back up and confidently straighten that crown as you rise. Embrace your imperfections and remember that it is through these moments of vulnerability that true strength and resilience are forged. So, go ahead and permit yourself to take a break, but always remember to reclaim your power and continue on your path with unwavering confidence.

Keep your head held high. You must maintain a confident and dignified posture, as it exudes strength and commands respect. Remember, queens are meant to rule with grace and poise, and holding your head high is a powerful way to assert your dominance. So, go forth with your head held high, queen, and conquer the world with your presence. The world is yours!

Part Four

Poetry from a Broken Heart

Made A Fool

I tried to understand,
but I ended up feeling more hurt.
I thought that you loved me
and knew what I was worth.

You treated me like a queen.
Put me on a pedestal.
Just to step out on me,
and have me looking like a fool.

My heart is aching.
The pain just won't go away.
I wanted to love you,
but after this, I cannot stay.

I sit in a trance,
trying to figure out where I went wrong.
You played me for a fool.
It's been going on for too long.

You denied knowing me

and denied me as your wife.
Why would you ever marry me,
and claim we would build a life?

A life together.
Just you and I.
With all of our children.
Until the day we die.

Your vows were a lie.
Our relationship has no truth.
You never really loved me.
You have no couth.

As I picked up the pieces
and mend my heart,
just know that I would have held you down.
I would have owned my part.

There were no limitations,
on what I would have done,
but you chose to step out,
and chose to have fun.

For the pain hurts now,
but this too shall stop.
Just give me some time.
I always come out on top.

True Colors

I remember the day I met you,
and what we talked about the first time we spoke.
You asked if I wanted to hang out,
and I still have all of your notes.

You spoke kind words
and always opened my door.
You kept me interested,
and I wanted to know more.

True colors started to show.
The more time passed by,
but I ignored the red flags,
and believed all your lies.

Things only got worse.
When I said there was a baby on the way.
The man I once knew had changed,
but I still hoped we'd be okay.

We got into an altercation,

that got way outta hand.
You tried to kill your child,
but still, call yourself a man.

For some unknown reason,
I forgave you for what you've done.
I had hoped that you were sorry,
and our family could remain as one.

Your abuse only got worse,
with every chance that you got.
You belittled me every time you could,
and I can't count how many times we've fought.

Insult after insult,
always placing the blame on me.
I finally realized you'd never change,
and we can never be a family.

You wished your child was dead.
You hoped that I would die,
but now you sit and wonder,
why I'm not by your side.

I deserve better,
and I deserve respect.
You can blame yourself.
For that reason I left.

How Dare You

How dare you,
look me in the face and lie.
Then claim that you hate it.
every time you see me cry.

You're the reason for my tears,
and my broken heart.
How dare you blame me,
for the reason we are apart.

How dare you play the victim
and act like I was wrong.
I was made to look like a fool.
You played with me all along.

How dare you make me believe,
every word you ever spoke.
You always made me promises,
that gave me a sense of hope.

Hope that this was real,

and hope you were being true.
How dare you be the devil in disguise,
and show me someone other than the real you.

How dare you get mad,
because I finally see through your lies.
How about you tell the truth for once,
and stop trying to hide?

How dare you say I did not support you,
and that I didn't have your back.
When I've been your backbone this entire time,
and THAT is a fact!

How dare you question my loyalty!
How dare you question my love!
When you and I know damn well,
you are the only one I was thinking of!

How dare you think you could get away with this,
and just throw me in the dirt.
Now that the truth is finally out,
you wanna act like the one that is hurt.

How dare you think I deserved this.
I think I have been through enough.
Don't think that this will keep me down.
I've always been tough!

Pieces of My Heart

I finally trusted,
enough to believe,
that maybe a man,
really could love me.

There's a hole in my chest.
Where my heart used to be.
There are clouds in my sky,
since he gave up on me.

I opened my heart
and gave all my love.
Just to find out,
I wasn't enough.

The pieces are shattered
and scattered about.
I can't put it back together.
I can't figure it out.

The pain is deep

and doesn't let up.
My only hope now,
is the next man will think I'm enough.

My heart will heal,
as more time passes by.
The pain will stop.
So will the tears in my eyes.

My Knight

One day there will be someone,
that will decide not to leave.
I'll trust them with everything I have
& they will truly love me.

He will open my eyes
& show me a whole new world
& make me realize,
it was fate to be his girl.

He'll pick up all the pieces
& mend my broken heart.
He'll show his appreciation,
from the very start.

I'll be his forever & only.
The love of his life.
He will give me a ring
& make me his wife.

I'll realize why it never worked out

With any other man.
He will love me unconditionally
& be my number 1 fan.

He will be my rock
& be my best friend
He will love me forever,
forever till the end.

Not Your Time

Nothing's worse than finding a man,
that spits a good game.
He makes you believe everything
but he is the same.

No respect for women
and a cold ass heart.
You hate yourself for trusting him.
I wish you hadn't let this start.

Y'all were friends at first
But that one text changed your mind.
You thought just maybe he was the one,
but soon the truth about him you would find.

You thought he was a different man.
Much different from the rest,
but it turned out he was just a fake.
Now all your feelings you regret.

This man will never love you,
nor did he have respect,
but love is around the corner, I promise.
It's just not your time yet.

But You're Toxic for Me

I fell in love with your smile,
your heart and your charm,
but you scare me,
because you have a great chance to cause me harm.

Every time I'm with you,
all my worries disappear.
Everything feels so perfect,
every time you are near.

I long for your love.
I long for your touch.
Hours seem like days when you're gone.
I hate that I miss you so much.

When you are gone,
it's a different person I see
You have the potential to be great,
but you're toxic to me.

There are so many questions in my mind,

but I try to ignore them and let them be.
You have the potential to be great,
but you're toxic to me.

You deflect my concerns
and push the blame back on me.
You have the potential to be great,
But you're toxic for me.

Love bombing and deflecting.
and gaslighting too.
You have the potential to be great,
but this is what narcissists do.

Is this trauma from your past,
that you never cared to work through?
And then it turned into insecurities,
and altered the person you once knew?

Your insecurities cause doubt
and will cause unnecessary fights.
Clearly, you don't trust me,
but I don't know how to make it right.

I've asked you a few times,
but then you say you're not insecure,
but I beg to differ.
Let's review this once more.

You get jealous when I post,
a selfie of me
and instead of talking to me about it bothering you,
you went ahead and unfriended me.

Said you're too insecure,

to see me post a "sexy" picture of me
and you chose to protect yourself
and handle it "maturely".

You have double standards
and it's very clear to see.
You have the potential to be great,
but you're toxic to me.

Your jealous episodes
are like a flashback of the past.
All these insecurities,
Will not help our relationship last.

I need to leave.
and I need to let you go.
You have the potential to be great,
But you're toxic for me I know.

I guess I fell in love with potential,
but I can't force you to see.
You have the potential to be great,
but you're toxic to me!

I see red flags.
It's something I can't ignore.
This is all too familiar.
I've seen this all before.

Everything started great,
but it is all a disguise.
Here come those red flags
And out came the lies.

www.ingramcontent.com/pod-product-compliance
Lightning Source LLC
Chambersburg PA
CBHW051423150726
48000CB00005B/1927